i P a d

I0053947

The Instant Solution to Under-Using of iPad

Tablets Devices

Oliver Sam

Copyright © 2019 Oliver Sam

ISBN: 978-1-63750-210-5

Table of Contents

Introduction

Over-70 million cell phone users in the world especially in United States of America, United Kingdom, Germany, France, Italy, Canada, Australia, India, Spain, Africa and other European countries, African countries, Asian countries and lot more uses the iPad 2, iPad (3rd generation), iPad (4th generation), iPad Air, iPad Air 2, iPad Pro (12.9-inch), iPad Pro (9.7-inch), iPad (5th generation), iPad Pro (12.9-inch) (2nd generation), iPad Pro (10.5-inch), iPad (6th generation), iPad Pro (11-inch), iPad Pro (12.9-inch) (3rd generation), iPad Air (3rd generation) aren't just faster and more powerful than ever—they're also better at all of the things you use an iPad tablets for. Following this informative guide, you will get a gorgeously illustrated guide to the shortcuts, tips, and workarounds that will turn you into an iPad master very fast without much ado.

This easy-to-use book will also get you up to speed on all iOS 13 features, improved performance features and also this book information is simple enough for kids, adolescents, and adult even if they are dummies, seniors and experts in the computer and technology world...

The easy-to-follow steps in this book will help you manage, personalize, and communicate using your new [iPad] Tablets. You will discover how to do everything from setting up for the first time, importing and managing contacts, taking professional pictures, managing apps, shopping online and organize appointments using iCal, to taking and sharing pictures and downloading and listening to your favorite music.

It helps you accomplish everything from web browsing

to watching videos, fixing slow iPad issues, watching and streaming live TV for FREE, importing and exporting contacts, files, unlocking iPad, fixing iPad problems and lot more. You'll get up to speed on features no one talks about.

Pick up this beautiful full-color book and learn how to get the most out of your iPad Now!

CHAPTER 1

First Time Set Up

There is no need for connecting your brand-new iPad to your personal computer, as long as there is a mobile data connection designed for activation. As you end the set-up wizard, you may navigate back by tapping the back arrow at the top left-hand side of the screen and scroll further to another display by tapping another button at the top right-hand corner.

You can commence by pressing down the power button at the top edge of your brand-new iPad. You may want to keep it pressed down for about two seconds until you notice a vibration, meaning the iPad is booting up.

Once it boots up finally, you can start initial set up by

following the processes below;

- Swipe your finger over the display screen to start the set-up wizard.

- Choose the language of preference - English is usually at the top of the list, so there is no problem finding it. However, if you would like to apply a different language, scroll down to look for your desired language, and tap to select the preferred language.

- Choose your country - United States may be near the top of the list. If otherwise, scroll down the list and select the United States or any of your choice.

- You need to connect your iPad to the internet to start its activation. You can test this via a link with a Wi-Fi network. Locate the name of your available network in the list shown, and then tap on it to select it.

- Enter the Wi-Fi security password (you will generally find this written on your router, which is probably known as the WPA Key, WEP Key, or Password) and select Sign up. A tick indication shows you are connected, and a radio image appears near the top of the screen. The iPad will now start activation with Apple automatically. This may take some time!

- In case your iPad is a 4G version, you will be requested to check for updated internet configurations after inserting a new Sim card. You can test this anytime, so, for the present time, tap **Continue**.

- Location services will help you with mapping, weather applications, and more, giving you specific information centred wholly on what your location is. Select whether to use location service by tapping allow location services.

- You would now be requested to create **Touch ID,** which is Apple's fingerprint identification. **Touch ID** allows you to unlock your iPad with your fingerprint instead of your passcode or security password. To set up Tap Identification, put a finger or your thumb on the home button (but do not press it down!). To by-pass this for the moment, tap *setup Tap Identification later*.

- If you are establishing Touch ID, the tutorial instruction on the screen will walk you through the set-up process. Put your finger on the home button, then remove till the iPad has properly scanned your fingerprint. Whenever your print is wholly scanned, you will notice a screen letting you know that tap recognition is successful. Tap **Continue.**

- You will be requested to enter a passcode to secure

your iPad. If you create **Touch ID**, you must use a passcode if in any case your fingerprint isn't acknowledged. Securing your computer data is an excellent idea, and the iPad provides you with several options. Tap password option to choose your lock method.

- You can arrange a Custom Alphanumeric Code (that is a security password that uses characters and figures), a Custom Numeric Code (digit mainly useful, however, you can add as many numbers as you want!) or a 4-Digit Numeric Code (a high old college pin!). In case you didn't install or setup **Touch ID** you may even have an option not to add Security password. Tap on your selected Security option.

- I would recommend establishing a 4-digit numeric code, or Touch ID for security reasons but all optional setup is done likewise. Input your selected Security password using the keyboard.

- Verify your Security password by inputting it again. If the Password does not match, you'll be requested to repeat! If indeed they do match, you'll continue to another display automatically.

At this time of the set-up process, you'll be asked whether you have used an iPad before and probably upgrading it, you can restore all of your applications and information from an iCloud or iTunes backup by deciding on the best option. If this is your first iPad, you will have to get it started as new, yet, in case you are moving from Android to an iPad, you can transfer all your data by deciding and choosing the choice you want.

How to Restore iPad Back-up from iCloud or iTunes

If you want to restore your iPad from an iTunes back-up, you may want to connect to iCloud and have the latest version of iTunes installed on it. If you are ready to begin this process, tap **restore** from iTunes back-up on your iPad and connect it to your personal computer. Instructions about how to bring back your data can be followed on the laptop screen.

In case your old iPad was supported on iCloud, then follow the instructions below to restore your applications & data to your brand-new device:

- Tap *Restore* from iCloud back-up.
- Register with the **Apple ID** and Password that you

applied to your old iPad. If you fail to recollect the security password, there's a link that may help you reset it.

- The Terms & Conditions screen will show. Tap the links to learn about specific areas in details. When you are ready to proceed, select **Agree**.

- Your **iPad** will need some moments to create your **Apple ID** and hook up with the **iCloud server**.

- You will notice a summary of available backups to download. The most up-to-date backup will be observed at the very top, with almost every other reserve below it. If you want to restore from a desirable backup, tap the screen for *all backups* to see the available choices.

- Tap on the back-up you want to restore to start installing.

- A progress bar will be shown, providing you with

a demo of the advancement of the download. When the restore is completed, the device will restart.

- You would see a notification telling you that your iPad is updated effectively. Tap *Continue*.

- To complete the iCloud set up on your recently restored iPad, you should re-enter your iCloud (**Apple ID**) password. Enter/review it and then tap *Next*.

- You'll be prompted to upgrade the security information related to your *Apple ID*. Tap on any stage to replace your computer data, or even to bypass this option. If you aren't ready to do this, then tap *Next* button.

- **Apple pay** is Apple's secure payment system that stores encrypted credit or debit cards data on your device and making use of your iPad also with your fingerprint to make safe transaction online and with other apps. Select *Next* to continue.

- To *feature/add a card*, place it on a set surface and place the iPad over it, so the card is put in the camera framework. The credit card info will be scanned automatically, and you will be requested to verify that the details on display correspond with your card. You'll also be asked to enter the *CVV* (safety code) from the personal strip behind the card. If you choose (or the camera cannot recognize your cards), you can enter credit card information by hand by tapping the hyperlink. You could bypass establishing **Apple Pay** by tapping *create later*.

- Another screen discusses *iCloud keychain*, which is Apple's secure approach to sharing your preserved security password and payment information throughout all your Apple devices. You might use *iCloud security code* to validate your brand-new device and import present data, or you might be asked to continue registering your keychain if it's your first Apple device. In case you don't want to share vital data with other devices, you should go to *avoid iCloud keychain* or *don't restore passwords*.

- If you selected to set up your **Apple keychain**, you'll be notified to either use Security password (the same one you'd set up on your iPad) or produce a different code. If you're making use of your iCloud security code, you should put it on your iPad when prompted.

- This will confirm your ID when signing on to an iCloud safety code; a confirmation code will be delivered via SMS. You may want to hyperlink your smartphone text code (if you have never distributed one with Apple already) so that the code may be provided as a text. Then enter this code to your iPad if requested, then select *Next.*

- You'll then be asked to create **Siri**. *Siri* is your own digital personal associate, which might search the internet, send communications, and check out data in your device and a lot more, all without having to flick via specific apps. Choose to create Siri by tapping the choice or start Siri later to skip this task for now.

- To set up and create **SIRI**, you will need to speak several phrases to the iPad to review your conversation patterns and identify your voice.

- Once you say every term, a tick will be observed, showing that it's been known and comprehended.

Another phrase may indicate that you should read aloud.

- Once you've completed the five phrases, you will notice a display notifying that Siri has been set up correctly. Tap *Continue*.

- The iPad display alters the color balance to help make the screen show up naturally under distinctive light conditions. You can switch this off in the screen settings after the iPad has completed configuring it. Tap *continue* to continue with the setup.

- Has your iPad been restored? Tap begin to transfer your computer data to your brand-new iPad.

- You'll be prompted to ensure your brand-new iPad has enough power to avoid the device turning off in the process of downloading applications and information. Tap *OK* to verify this recommendation.

- You will notice a notification show up on your apps, to download in the background.

How to Move Data From Android

Apple has made it quite easy to move your data from a Google Android device to your new iPad. Proceed to the iOS app. I'll direct you about how to use the application to move your data!

- Using the iPad, if you are on the applications & data screen of the set-up wizard, tap *move data from Google android.*

- Go to the Play Store on your Google android device and download the app recommended by the set-up wizard. When it is installed, open up the app, select **Continue** and you'll be shown the *Terms &*

Conditions to continue.

- On your Android device, tap *Next* to start linking your Devices. On your own iPad, select *Continue*.

- Your iPad will show a 6-digit code which has to be received into the Google android device to set the two phone up.

- Your Google android device will screen all the data that'll be moved. By default, all options are ticked - so if there could be something you don't want to move, tap the related collection to deselect it. If you are prepared to continue, tap *Next* on your Google android device.

- As the change progresses, you will notice the iPad display screen changes, showing you the position of the info transfer and progress report.

- When the transfer is completed, you will notice a confirmation screen on each device. On your Android Device, select *Done* to shut the app. On your iPad, tap *Continue Installing iPad*.

- An **Apple ID** allows you to download apps, supported by your iPad and synchronize data through multiple devices, which makes it an essential account you should have on your iPad! If you have been using an iPad previously, or use iTunes to download music to your laptop, then you should have already become an **Apple ID user**. Register with your username and passwords (when you have lost or forgotten your **Apple ID** or password you will see a link that may help you reset it). If you're not used to iPad, select doesn't have an Apple ID to create one for free.

- The Terms & Conditions for your iPad can be seen.

Please go through them (tapping on more to study additional info), so when you are done, tap *Agree*.

- You'll be asked about synchronizing your data with iCloud. That's to ensure bookmarks, connections and other items of data are supported securely with your other iPad's data. Tap *merge* to permit this or *don't merge* if you'll have a choice to keep your details elsewhere asides iCloud.

- **Apple pay** is Apple's secure payment system that stores encrypted credit or debit cards data on your device and making use of your iPad also with your fingerprint to make safe transaction online and with other apps. Select *Next* to continue.

- To *feature/add a card*, place it on a set surface and place the iPad over it, so the card is put in the camera framework. The credit card info will be scanned automatically, and you will be requested to verify that the details on display correspond with your card. You'll also be asked to enter the *CVV* (safety code) from the personal strip behind the card. If you choose (or the camera cannot recognize your cards), you can enter credit card information by hand by tapping the hyperlink. You could bypass establishing **Apple Pay** by tapping *create later*.

- Another screen discusses *iCloud keychain*, which is Apple's secure approach to sharing your preserved security password and payment information throughout all your Apple devices. You might use *iCloud security code* to validate your brand-new device and import present data, or you might be asked to continue registering your keychain if it's your first Apple device. In case you don't want to share vital data with other devices, you should go to *avoid iCloud keychain* or *don't restore passwords*.

- If you selected to set up your Apple keychain, you'll be notified to either use Security password (the same one you'd set up on your iPad) or produce a different code. If you're making use of your iCloud security code, you should put it on your iPad when prompted.

- This will confirm your ID when signing on to an iCloud safety code; a confirmation code will be delivered via SMS. You may want to hyperlink your smartphone text code (if you have never distributed one with Apple already) so that the code may be provided as a text. Then enter this code to your iPad if requested, then select **Next.**

- You'll then be asked to create **Siri**. *Siri* is your own digital personal associate, which might search the internet, send communications, and check out data in your device and a lot more, all without having to flick via specific apps. Choose to create Siri by tapping the choice or start Siri later to skip this task for now.

- To set up and create SIRI, you will need to speak several phrases to the iPad to review your conversation patterns and identify your voice.

- Once you say every term, a tick will be observed, showing that it's been known and comprehended. Another phrase may indicate that you should read aloud.

- Once you've completed the five phrases, you will notice a display notifying that Siri has been set up correctly. Tap *Continue*.

- The iPad display alters the color balance to help make the screen show up naturally under distinctive light conditions. You can switch this off in the screen settings after the iPad has completed configuring it. Tap *continue* to continue with the setup.

- Has your iPad been restored? Tap begin to transfer your computer data to your brand-new iPad.

- You'll be prompted to ensure your brand-new iPad has enough power to avoid the device turning off in the process of downloading applications and information. Tap **OK** to verify this recommendation.

- You will notice a notification show up on your apps, to download in the background.

NB: Setting up as new iPad: Similar method, as described above, applies.

How To Add Email Account(s)

The iPad allows multiple POP3, IMAP, and other accounts. If you have one email, take into account one for work and another one for private/home, getting all of your emails is as simple as adding every of the account on your iPad.

- To commence, select the *Configurations icon.*

- In the configurations, find and tap on Email, on another page, tap on Account to add.

- At the right-hand side, tap **ADD ACCOUNT**.

- Choose your E-mail providers (e.g. Google, Yahoo, Live, etc...) from the list shown. Mail Accounts is often utilized by companies and network service providers, live.com is the new name for a Hotmail or windows live accounts, and YAHOO!, GOOGLE and AOL are self-explanatory. For another e-mail company, select **OTHER** followed by tapping *ADD Email Account*.

- Review your **EMAIL** and Security password (aside from some other data required, alongside your name) as asked, and Tap **Next** or **Register** on the screen to continue.

- If the account(s) is established, you may review your details was successfully founded, or a data screen about how exactly your e-mail accounts can be utilized. You might allow this or tap **Next** to continue.

- This may then automatically spread to show notifications to be able to pick and choose which data the accounts will use on your new iPad - email, connections, calendars, and probably different items too, with regards to the accounts. *Turn OFF* notifications for just about any items you do not need to be on your iPad, then select

Save.

- Once completed, you should see your accounts in the list at the right-hand part of the screen.

In case your e-mail account does not install or get created, you'll be requested for additional information regarding the account, which includes incoming email server settings. You might contact them simultaneously for help. Once you've introduced your accounts, you could gain access to your email messages by tapping the email icon on your home screen. When you have installed several electronic mail accounts, you might view all your emails in a single inbox by selecting the *ALL INBOXES* option from the mailbox section in the e-mail app.

Sending Emails & Attachments from iPad

To send an email, you ought to have already created an email account on your iPad.

- Find and open the app on your home display screen. This looks like a White Envelope, and if you've acquired emails already, there may be a pink badge on it which represents some unread email messages.

- The email App will open up your brand-new E-mail. To view your inbox, Tap **INBOX or ALL INBOXES** at the top left-hand nook of the screen.

- When you can see your E-mail inbox, select the **COMPOSE BUTTON**. This looks like a pen and paper, and it's located at the top-right nook of the email inbox screen.

- The screen will now show blank email, ready to begin writing.

- New emails will regularly send from your default electronic mail account (which is usually the first one you have added). When you have multiple accounts on your iPad and want to switch the accounts to send from, it is easy to do. Touch the **CC/BCC, FROM** collection which shows the e-mail address with which you're sending from, then Touch the e-mail address shown to change it to another account.

- To add a **recipient**, Tap into the **TO** field. To browse your contact list, Tap the + button at the right-hand aspect of the display. You could additionally start to type their name, and any matching contacts would be shown allowing you to pick the one you are searching out for. In case you don't have the Tap saved for your device already, simply Tap the **TO** Field and start typing the E-mail address you wish to send to.

- Utilize the **SUBJECT** box to add a title to your e-mail.

- Tap into the main window (above the pre-loaded send from my iPad signature) to put the cursor there and type your message. When you're ready to send your e-mail, select **Send** at the top right-hand nook.

How to Add an Attachment to E-Mail

iPads can feature photos and videos from the device as an attachment ever since iOS 7 was launched in 2013. However, you can now additionally add attachments from online storage including Google Drive or Dropbox, especially with the recent **iOS 13, iOS 12 and iOS versions** to come.

How to Attach an Image or Video From Your iPad

- Begin by creating and accessing your email account as stated above.

- To feature/attach a picture or video, Tap the **CAMERA** icon to the right of the keyboard's top level.

- Please navigate through the image folders you've created for your iPad to discover the image or video you want to transfer and Tap it to choose it.

- To choose the image or video and connect it for your email, Tap **USE**. You can attach one at a time. However, nothing is stopping you from adding any other one!

- Provided that you've launched your internet connection, Tap **SEND** to get it sent immediately.

How to Add a Document From an Online Storage App

To add accessories from a web storage account such as **Dropbox or Google Drive**, you'll need to have the App for that service installed on your iPad and be signed directly into your account in the App to gain access to your documents.

- Create your email as described above, then select the paper clip icon to the right of the keyboard's top line.

- By default, your **iCloud Drive Storage** will open. If that is where your file is, navigate through your folders and choose it. To import an item from external storage, Tap **SOURCE**.

- The first time you use this feature, you'll want to

allow access to which you will use an option storage space source. Tap **More**.

- The manage location display allows you to select the storage Apps you want to include documents from elsewhere. Tap the switch to the right of your preferred App to allow/enable it (it turns green) then Tap **DONE**.

- You'll then be back at the **iCloud Drive Screen**. Tap Source once more to open up your storage choices.

- This time all the storage space Apps you enabled in the previous display screen should be accessible for you in the menu. Tap the Appropriate one to discover the files and folders therein.

- Please navigate through the folders to locate the file you are considering, and Tap it to attach it to your email.

- When you've attached your document(s), Tap **SEND**

to get document attached and sent to your contact(s)!

CHAPTER 2

How To Fix iPad Email that does not Work

Among the predominant benefits of the iPad is it will keep you connected to almost anybody from anywhere. Whether it's by text, social press, or e-mail, your iPad is your marketing communications lifeline to the world. That is one of the things that makes it so irritating whenever your e-mail is no longer working (it's so annoying if you would like to get an electronic email for your business or job).

You'll find so many issues that could affect your iPad form downloading e-mail, which explains why this section is entirely for you if you're confronted with email challenges.

You will find eight predominant steps you might use to try and solve the majority of the challenges you might be facing with e-mail.

We shall start highlighting them individually.

- **Check Your Network Connection**

Your iPad cannot get an e-mail if it's not linked to the internet. It's essential to get access to a mobile network through your phone or a Wi-Fi network that may grant you access to e-mail.

You need to additionally ensure that Airplane mode is not enabled on your iPad because that could quickly block contacts to mobile and Wi-Fi networks.

- **Restart Your Email App**

One quick way to repair any application not operating as

anticipated is to exit and re-launch the application. That is another simple method of solving mail difficulties. To try out this method, follow the next steps:

1.   Double select your iPad Home button.

2.   When the multi-tasking view shows up, find Mail.

3.   Swipe Email up and close the display.

4.   Click once on the Home button.

5.   Tap the Mail application to re-launch it.

- **Restart Your iPad**

If regardless your web connection is intact and you've restarted the email app, and you also see that the problem persists, the next step is one of the most typical in every **iPad-troubleshooting guide** which is to restart your smartphone.

Sometimes it's hard for individuals to trust because we

always expect that organic approach must be employed to solving problems; however, in most instances, a simple method usually is our best bet. So; restarting an iPad can get rid of loads of issues. Sometimes your mobile phone needs a new start-up.

- **Upgrade Your iPad iOS version**

Among the top method of troubleshooting is to ensure you have the latest version of the iOS working on your device. An updated version of the iOS fixes bugs in today's version on your phone automatically and update its functions. Practically, the problems with your e-mail is a harmful bug program which can best be set with the latest iOS upgrade or your e-mail provider has made a few changes to their configurations, and it's only the latest iOS version to guide you to cope with the change.

- **Delete, and Set-up E-mail Accounts Again**

If none of the steps enumerated above solved the issue, there might not be anything wrong with your iPad. On the other hand, the problem can also be from the configurations used to try reference to your Email accounts. Perhaps; if you enter a wrong server address, username, or security password when establishing the accounts on your iPad, you might not be capable of getting an Email.

If this is the case, you can begin once more by deleting the e-mail accounts from your mobile phone following a few steps below:

1. Head to Settings.

2. Go directly to the Tabs where you see Email, Contacts, and Calendar.

3. Go through the accounts with the problem.

4. Delete the Accounts.

5.   Delete from My iPad in the pop-up menu in the bottom of the screen.

Having deleted the e-mail accounts, check all the settings that you can use to gain access to this accounts and feel the procedure of adding an e-mail account in your iPad again (you might synchronize the reports to your phone through iTunes).

There are many other ways of deleting an email account from an iPad; this and many other important information would be explained explicitly in a later edition of this book.

- **Contact Email Provider**

As of this juncture, it's time to get some excellent direct technical support for your e-mail issues.

An excellent approach is to check with your e-mail provider, such as (Google for Gmail, Yahoo, and many more.). Each Email service provider has specific ways to provide support; however, a great strategy is to log into your email accounts on the internet through a pc and then navigate to your company support link.

- **Make an Apple Store Appointment**

In case your email provider can't help, you might have a problem that is complex than you are designed for. If so, it is the best shot that you should take your iPad-and all the info about the e-mail account-to the nearest Apple Store for tech support team (you could additionally call Apple for support). Apple stores are usually occupied, so be sure to make a scheduled appointment before moving out to avoid waiting around all day long at their offices.

- **Check Your IT Department**

If regardless you're trying to check a work Email

accounts, and if the first five steps didn't work, it is most possible that the problem doesn't tally with your iPad whatsoever. The problem may be from the email server you want to download email from. When there is a brief concern with that server or a construction change that you aren't aware, that could impact and stop your iPad from being able to access it. So if the e-mail account is from your workplace, I'll recommend you contact and talk with the IT division for a solution.

CHAPTER 3

Adding & Importing Contact to iPad

When you have contacts on your old smartphone or device that you'll like to import to your brand-new iPad, please don't be worried I'll guide you!

Using Apple's iCloud service, you'll be able to import storage space documents and synchronize contacts simultaneously to your iPad.

If you have formerly been using an iPad, then transferring your contacts would be more comfortable by using **_Apple's iCloud Online Sync Service._**

In case your old mobile device has been installed to use iCloud, then your use of the same Apple identity (ID) on your iPad will deliver your contacts, calendar, and other information right to your brand-new device with no need for further action.

If you don't have iCloud installed on your old iPad, then it's the very first thing you will need to configure. Your old iPad should be associated with a Wi-Fi network so that people can reproduce or duplicate the info from your mobile phone to iCloud.

Do the following on your old iPad:

- Locate and tap the Configurations icon.

- Scroll down and select *iCloud*.

- If you see your address at the very top line, this means you're authorized directly into iCloud on your old iPad. If not, subscribe with the same Apple ID that you've used for your brand-new iPad.

- Turn internet network **ON.**

- Select the choice to Merge your computer data with **iCloud**. This will add all of your contacts to iCloud.

When you have already passed the initial set up the stage for your iPad, you might activate the iCloud services following precise instructions as stated above. When you're connected directly to iCloud, your contacts will start to download to your brand-new iPad immediately. If you have configured your old iPad to the iCloud service, all you have to do is select the option to use iCloud through the initial set up of your **iPad**, as well as your contacts that will automatically show up on these devices.

How to Import Contacts From a Blackberry Phone

To control your Blackberry contacts, we first need to transfer these to your computer. To do this, you must first download and set up the blackberry laptop software. As the software is installed, adhere to the instructions below!

- Connect your Blackberry to your laptop by using a micro USB cable for Blackberry processing device computer software to comprehend and identify the smartphone.

- Select Organizer at the left-hand panel of the program and tick the contacts field.

- While requested to choose the Sync Path, choose your laptop/computer only.

- Below contacts account, be sure home windows contacts is chosen. Press **OK** to continue.

- Press sync organizer at the right-hand part of the program to move your Blackberry contacts onto your home windows address book.

- Given that your contacts are saved in windows contacts, you can synchronize these details to your iPad through the iTunes software. If you have not already installed iTunes, download it from Apple's download website, making sure that your iPad isn't associated with your personal computer when you install the program.

- If iTunes is currently installed on your pc, connect your iPad through the provided USB cable and go through the Info Tabs near the top of the summary web page.

- Given that you're at the information tab, you will notice a tick box to Synchronize Your Contacts. Make sure that iTunes is defined to synchronize with your windows contacts; tick the package and press synchronize at the bottom left part of iTunes.

- Your contacts will now be shown on your iPad! If you have signed directly into iCloud on your mobile phone, your contacts will now start copying to Apple's cloud storage space service.

How to Import Contacts from a Windows Phone

To transfer contacts from a windows phone to your iPad, you'd first move the contacts to your home windows contacts program on your laptop. That is a reasonably reliable method, and also to learn more, keep reading!

- If you're migrating from a home windows phone and your mobile phone is linked to the internet, you ought to have Home windows Live (or

Hotmail) accounts already created on the smartphone. Under these events, your contacts can be stored on the Home windows live website by default. Go through the link and register with your home windows e-mail address and security password when prompted.

- Once you can see your contacts list, click a button near the top of the web page and choose Export from the dropdown list. Your contacts will begin installing as a .csv file on your personal computer.

- On your PC, go through the start menu and open up contacts.

- From the very best of the connection's windows, press import and choose CSV as your selected file type. Press import to save.

- Go through the search button to get the downloaded duplicate of your home windows live contacts. Once you've located it, press Next to start importing the contacts to your laptop's address folder.

- Given that your contacts are kept in windows contacts, you would be able to synchronize this data to your iPad through the iTunes program. If you haven't already downloaded iTunes from Apple's download web page, please do.

- If iTunes is currently established on your pc, connect your iPad via the provided USB cable and go through the *INFO* tabs near the top of the summary web page.

- Given that you're at the info tab, you will notice a tick-box to sync your contacts. Affirm that iTunes is defined to synchronize with your Home windows contacts, tick the field and press *SYNCHRONIZE* in the bottom left part of iTunes.

- Your contacts will now show up on your iPad! If you've signed on directly into iCloud on your mobile phone, your contacts will now start backing up just as much as Apple's cloud storage space service is enabled.

How to Import Contacts From A Google Android To iPad

Your Android device can export its contacts into a storage space file, the precise form of a written report which iCloud has is with the capacity of managing and absorbing. Once your links are in iCloud, it is only a matter of time expecting the info to complete synchronizing on your iPad. However, if you are uncertain how to actualize this stage, then examine the steps below to discover more!

If the contacts aren't on the Google account on your old

Android device, we'll need to get them there so that you can transfer these to your iPad, so that you will need to focus on step one as described below. If the contacts are already in your Google accounts, you may ignore this step.

To migrate your contacts out of your old Android device to your Google accounts:

- On your Android phone, tap the Contacts icon on your home display, or within the programs list.

- Tap the menu key, both as a button below the screen with three lines or the display screen button at the top-right corner, with three dots icon.

- Tap **Import/Export**. Several Android phones need you to press *More* before you start to see the *import/export settings.*

- Tap *Export to SDCARD*, or *Export to Storage Space* depending on your mobile phone.

- When exported and you're back viewing the contacts list, select the *menu key* again.

- Tap *Import/export,* as done in the third step.

- Tap import from **SDCARD** or *import from Storage space* depending on your mobile phone.

- If you are asked where to import the contacts to, tap Google or the Google E-mail address.

- Based on your specific phone, you'll be requested to choose which contacts to import. If so, pick all links. Your links will now be on your Google accounts!

Given that your contacts are on your Google accounts, you will extract these details and stick it onto the iCloud accounts such that it synchronizes to your iPad.

- On your laptop, head to Google's contacts website and subscribe with your Google email and password.

- From your Google contact, near the top of your contacts, press *More*, and consequently *Export*.

- Ensure that the all contacts radio field is ticked, in addition to memory cards format- Press *Export* to download your contacts on your computer.

- From your laptop's web browser, go to the iCloud website and register to make use of your Apple ID and Password.

- Go through the Contacts, a summary of all your contacts presently residing on your **iCloud account**.

- Press the configurations icon in the bottom-left part of the contacts page. This appears as though it's a cog or tool.

- From your menu which shows up, go through the import button, and navigate to your download folder. After picking your cards to import and Press Okay, your contacts will begin to show in iCloud! Within a few minutes, your iPad will start to show the same contacts too.

How to Add Contact to Your iPad Tablets Manually

We have discussed uploading your contacts from your previous device; however, when you begin using your device, you will want to add contacts as you go and edit or update the info of individuals you already have. Don't worry; you will become familiar with that now.

How to Add a New Contact

To include a completely new contact on your iPad, follow the instructions described below:

- Tap on the Contact App on your home Display.

- You might see any previously existing contacts on your display. To include a brand-new contact, select the blue+ at the very top right-hand nook.

- Enter the name of your brand-new contact in the areas supplied near the top of the screen. To add a mobile number, tap **add mobile**. Tap where it says Telephone to input the number, and you'll change the label home to a choice of yours by tapping it and selecting your desired from a list. To include an electronic email address, tap add E-mail, so that as you scroll down, you might see areas for additional input information, comprising home address, birthday, or even established custom ringtones and message shades for the contact.

- If you are satisfied with the info you have in your brand-new contact, tap *completed* at the very top right-hand nook to save the contact.

- Tap All Contacts at the very top left-hand nook to go again to your contact list.

Once you have stored your contact, select + to feature or add every other or tap the home button to come back to your home screen.

How to Edit iPad Contact

Editing a contact on your iPad isn't expected to vary from including a new one, just can be seen barely in yet another way.

To edit a contact:

- Open up the Contacts application from the home

display.

- Please scroll down and select the contact you want to edit, to open up it.

- At the very top right-hand corner, tap *Edit*.

- Now you can edit the contact's details as explained above, adding or changing the info as required. If you want to delete any data from a contact, select the pink group icon left of the sphere and tap delete at the right of the range.

If you wish to delete the contact completely, scroll downwards and select ***delete the contact***.

CHAPTER 4

How to Secure iPad with Lock Screen

On an iPad, you have a preference among a Custom Alphanumeric Code (that is a password with the use of letters and numbers), a Custom Numeric Code (figures only, however as many digits as you prefer!) or a 4-Digit Numeric Code (a fantastic old style pin!). You will need to decide which you need to use, so it is worth considering that earlier than you dive into the settings.

- Tap on the configuration icon, then scroll down and Tap on *Touch ID & Password*.

- In the **Touch ID** & Password menu, tap the blue hyperlink to turn Password ON.

- The default Security password placing is a Custom Alphanumeric Code - a complex password containing letters and digits. You could alternate this by tapping Password options.

- Tap your chosen password option to select it.

- Enter your **PASSWORD**. While you type in your secret four-digit, the display screen will increase automatically.

- Re-input your Security password to verify it. If the entered Passwords do not match, you might be returned to the first Security password access display to start over. If the Password that has been entered matches, then you will go back to the Security password menu.

- The final element to decide is how fast you want to enter your Password, which is often a balance between usability and safety. To change this setting, Tap **Require Password**.

- Pick your time out from the listing on screen by

tapping the interval you want to set. A tick will appear on that line, and when you're happy with the setting, tap Back at the very top left-hand nook.

You can allow access to certain functions of your iPad when the screen is locked. There are switches to enable the usage of *NOTIFICATIONS, SIRI*, and other components of the working gadget. Tap any of these to permit them (when **ON**, the switches can look green).

How to Set Up Touch ID to Unlock Your iPad

Now that you have set up a Password, you may want to enable **Touch ID**, which is fingerprint recognition to unlock your Devices (meaning you might not need to type in that password, even though you could if you want to!).

Follow the instructions below to achieve this effortlessly;

- To begin setting up **Touch ID**, you will want to be within the Settings **Menu**.

- In the predominant settings menu, select **Touch ID & Password.**

- Input your **Password** to access the settings.

- Tap **Add a Fingerprint**.

- To start including your fingerprint, place your finger or thumb onto the *Home button*, however, do not press it. Lift and replace your finger as instructed on-screen, shifting it very slightly as you achieve this. When the center of your fingerprint has been scanned, you'll be requested to place your finger in unique positions on the home button to experiment the edges.

- While your fingerprint is fully scanned, you will

see the whole screen, displaying that your print has been captured and Touch ID is ready. Touch **Continue**.

- As you add fingerprints, they'll be numbered. You can change the names (so you recognize which print is which) or delete fingerprints from the phone by Tapping the name after which editing or deleting as required.

- When you've modified the name of fingerprint, Tap **Done** on the keyboard to keep the new name.

- **TOUCH ID** will be without delay activated for unlocking your iPad, and for **Apple Pay**. To enable iTunes and App Store Purchases to be authorized alongside with your fingerprint, Tap the switch to carefully turn it **ON,** then get into your Apple ID password.

You can upload as much as five Fingerprints, so putting

in place fingerprint access for your family members may be carried out too. A phrase of warning though; remember that in case you've introduced the capacity to use fingerprint scanning to authorize iTunes and App Store buys, anybody who's fingerprint is added can do this too!

CHAPTER 5

Setting up Wi-Fi & Mobile Networks

Would you like to connect your iPad to the internet before you begin the utilization of several features, like email and the application store? Right here is a way for connecting your iPad to a guaranteed wireless network as well as your mobile data network for access to the internet.

You might have recently been linked to Wi-Fi through the preliminary iPad setup, however, if you didn't, or want to get on a particular wireless network, then this section of the manual is the correct one for you!

How to Connect Your iPad to Mobile Data

If you procure your iPad on a promo, you might in all probability have a month data bundle incorporated with the agreement. Allowing you to apply the internet if you are far-away from any Wi-Fi systems. This is set up automatically when you initially start your iPad, and that means you should manage to connect anywhere as long as there's a stable mobile network transmission strength! If this is not the situation, follow my brief steps below to discover the best way to get the mobile internet ready for use.

- From the home display, Tap on the configuration icon.

- In the predominant configurations listing, tap on Mobile data (depending on your network, you might see Cellular data as an alternative).

- Ensure the *Mobile data* is defined **ON** (green),

tapping the change to allow it if required.

- If this hasn't worked well, you might enter configurations manually for your unique network operator. To get into these configurations, scroll right down to Mobile data network and tap on it to gain access to an option generally called *APN*.

- You could additionally have the ability to re-download the configurations from your Sim card by scrolling to the low area of the APN configurations website and tap reset configurations.

- If none of the strategies gets you connected to a mobile data network, I would suggest contacting your mobile network issuer for additional help, as they are capacitated to sending the configurations without delay to your device from their end.

I'd suggest most effectively the utilization of Mobile internet for email messages and general web surfing. If you watch many movies or pay attention to many online pieces of music, you might use your computer data bundle very quickly and turn into getting billed extra sums in addition to your month-to-month invoice. Test with your network service provider to discover your computer data charge, and look at the telephone bill app to know your recent data for each month.

Connecting Your iPad to a Wi-Fi network

For connecting your iPad to a Wi-Fi network, you'll first need to find the security key for the network. This may be on the sticker at the back or source of your router, and it might be called a WEP Key, WPA Key, or Wi-Fi password. If you're uncertain, you could check up on the person that installs your network, or your web service provider.

When you have this data, you are equipped to start!

- From the home display screen, tap on the configuration's icon.

- Within the settings menu, select *Wi-Fi*.

- Make sure the WiFi switch is preparing to *ON* (green) if it's not from inception, tap the change to *enable/allow* it. Using the WiFi *ON*, your iPad will check out and screen all available systems. Choose your network's name from the list shown and tap on it.

- When prompted, enter the *Wi-Fi* security password. That is delicate, so be sure you don't mistype it, so when you are ready to continue, tap **Join**.

- When the iPad is installed to the network, you might visit a blue tick shown up on the network's name, and a radio image will be observed next to your mobile network's name at the very top level of the screen. Whenever your iPad is at the range of the network, and wireless is switched **ON**, it'll connect automatically.

Enabling and Disabling the iPad Internet Connection

How to Turn OFF your Wireless Connection

If your wireless connection is slow, you may want to turn it off for a short time to let you use mobile data as a substitute - be aware of lots of information you are probable to apply! Apple has made it very quick and smooth to do this.

Open Control Centre by swiping up from below the Display Screen. In Control Centre you will see a row of six spherical icons which might be White when the function is turned **ON** and Gray while it's **OFF**. The Wi-Fi image must be the second icon from the left, so tap this to put it out.

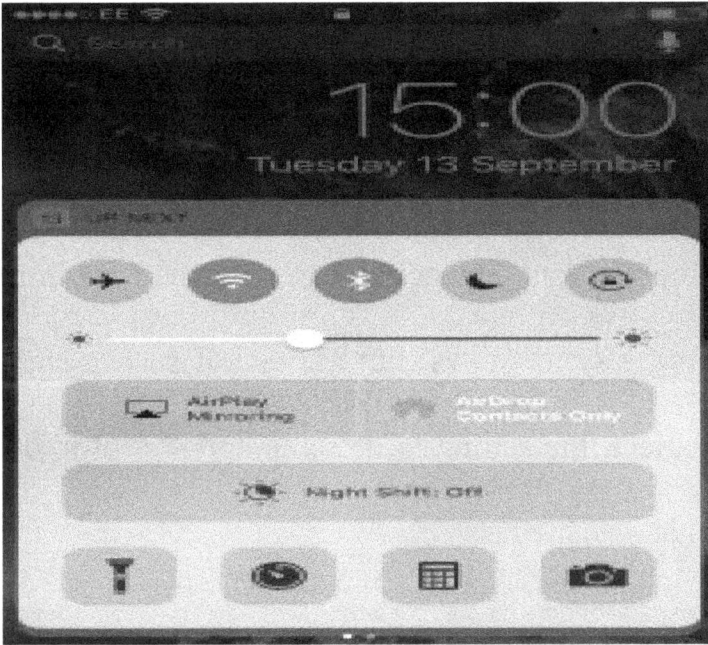

As soon as you have completed that, the wireless symbol next on your network name at the top of the display will disappear, displaying you're no longer linked to the internet. In case your iPad has a Sim card in it, the wireless image will be replaced by the data connection indicator (4G, 3G, E, GPRS) and you will be back again on Mobile Network. Just do not forget to turn your

Wireless ON back to keep away from those pesky data charges!

How to Turn OFF Mobile Data

Your mobile data connection can be turned off in much the same way as Wi-Fi, but as it's not such a standard requirement, the setting to do so is buried a little deeper in the handset menus.

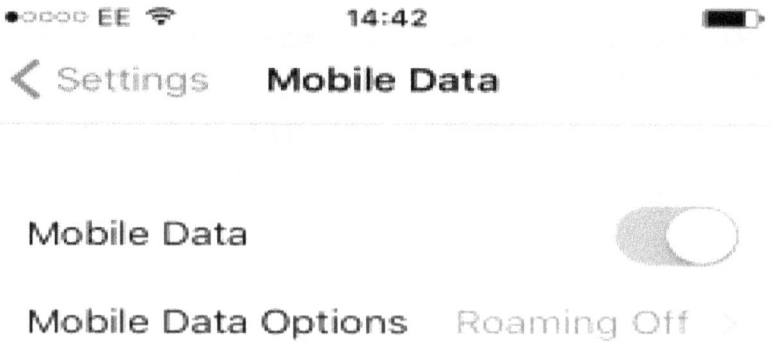

●○○○○ EE 🛜   14:42   ▬▬▭

‹ Settings   **Mobile Data**

Mobile Data   ⬭

Mobile Data Options   Roaming Off ›

1.   From the Home screen, locate and tap on Settings.

2.   In the top section of the main settings menu, select on Mobile or Cellular (you would see one word or the

other, depending on your mobile network).

3.   At the top of the Mobile Data menu, there is a switch for Mobile Data. When enabled, the switch shows green. To turn off your data connection, tap the change. With your data connection turned off, your phone will only access the internet if you connect to a Wi-Fi network.

CHAPTER 6

How To Use App Store To Find Applications

Do you want to download apps to your iPad? With such a lot to choose from in the app store, it's hard to realize where to begin! Right here's the way to get the tasty morsels of application from the Apple application store for your iPad.

How to Download New App on iPad

Downloading new applications via the app store is a reasonably direct process; however, when you download your first app, you can have a bit of set up to do in regards to your **Apple ID**. Comply with the instructions underneath, and you will have your iPad ever downloading apps right away!

- To begin, tap the App Store icon at the home screen of your new iPad.

- The store will open up with the Featured Apps web page. This may display to you the applications presently being promoted, either by Apple themselves or via the App developers. You can scroll down the page to look at distinct sections, and each areas' icons can be swiped through to examine which apps are being featured.

- Tapping **See All** at the right-hand side of every featured segment will show you that option in more detail.

- At the top left of the first website, you could select on **Categories**, which breaks up the App Store into broadly titled segments, without difficulty navigating through the sections. Tap **Cancel** at the top to return to the presented apps web page.

- In the categories, you may see sub-categories to make it simpler to browse the kind of apps you're looking for.

- At the bottom of the leading web page, you'll find links to various sections of the App Store. Featured you will see, and top Charts which are self-explanatory - brief access to **"Top 40 applications"** style lists of free and paid applications if you want to scroll through.

Explore allows you to look for what human nearby are downloading, which can be quite useful when trying to find your way around a new location, or in case you're at a sporting or musical occasion.

Tapping **SEARCH** at the lower part of the display screen allows you to enter the name of an App you have heard about or recommended to you.

Updates, as the name implies, is where you can control

your apps and download updates.

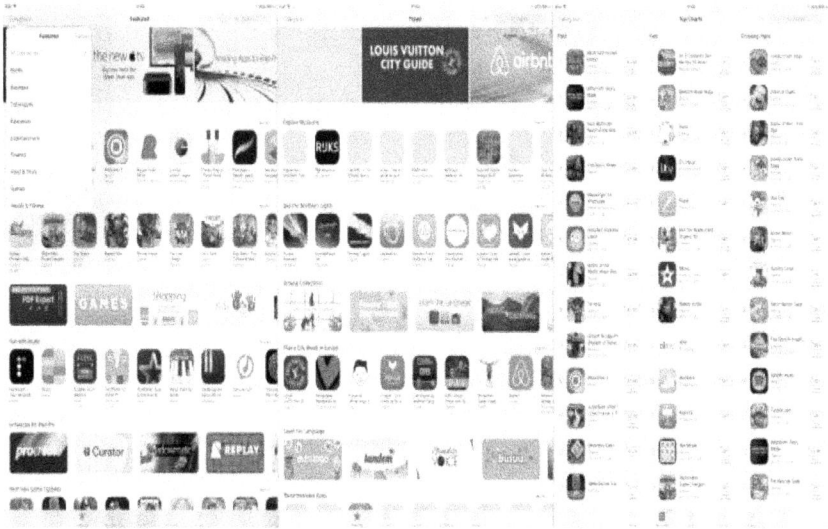

- When using the search function, anything you type into the field causes results to auto-fill on the web page. Tap the Search suggestion you like, to see what apps it brings up.

- If the button to the right-hand side of the app's name says **Download**, the app is free, and there will be no price to yourself. Tapping the word **Download** will change the box to say **Install**.

- Tapping Install will start the download process. If there is a fee, the price would be displayed in place of the term **Download**, and you'll be asked to link a card to your **Apple ID** to pay for this and any future purchases.

- If that is the first app you have attempted to download on your new iPad, you may be requested to input your **Apple ID** information. If you have already got an **Apple ID** (if this is your first iPad you will be prompted to create one at some stage in the initial set up process), you can tap use existing **Apple ID**, and **Sign in**. In case you do not have an Apple ID, select create a new Apple ID and observe the on-screen instructions to create your free Apple ID account. When you have already introduced your Apple ID by signing into iCloud, you will need to put in your password.

- For ease of use, you may set a time hold of 15 or more minutes before your password is needed again. This can make it smooth to install several apps in one session as you may not need to enter your password every time. Tap to regularly require your security password or require after 15 minutes, as you deem fit to you.

- You'll necessarily need to accept the iTunes Terms & Conditions, and the Apple privacy policy (which you can get dispatched to yourself via email by tapping the supplied hyperlink) by tapping **Agree**, then show that you genuinely do agree by tapping **Agree** again!

- With your account signed in and the agreements handled, your app can now be downloaded. Tap ok for this to happen.

- When the application is downloading, you'll see a

blue development indicator in the shape of a circle, with a square at the middle. Tap this if you want to pause/restart the download for any cause.

- When the application has been successfully installed, the progress button changes to an open button to which will let you access the app. When installing, the app will also appear in the first available home display area. However, you can without difficulty move this in case you want!

While you've completed your task in the store, press the **Home button** at the bottom of the iPad's front panel to return to your home display screen. Swipe across to see your newly installed apps!

How to Manage Apps on iPad
How to re-arrange iPad Apps

Whenever you download a brand-new app, it is automatically going to primarily occupy the next available space on your home display. You can easily re-arrange the applications into any order you want. To try this, tap and hold your finger on the application icon for some seconds. All the icons start jiggling. Now, all you want to do is place your finger on the image you need to move and drag it to the precise position of your choice. You can walk in between the display screen by moving the icon at the edge of the screen for a 2nd or 3rd. When you have finished, press the home button to go back to the standard display.

How to Organize iPad Folders

Setting your apps in folders makes it loads quickly to search out the app you're searching. In preference to scrolling through pages of apps, you could click on the appropriate folder and go immediately to the app you want.

To create a folder, all you need to do is place your finger on an app icon until it starts to jiggle similarly to when you are re-arranging apps. Then pull and drop an application icon at the top of another app icon. This will place both applications in a folder. You may change the name of the folder and move in a few more apps if you need. If you have completed the process, press the home button.

To move objects out of a folder, open up the folder first

then maintain your finger on one of the application icons in it until they jiggle, then tap and hold on your selected app, and drag it out of the folder to the home screen. If you pull the remaining last app out of the folder, the folder itself will vanish.

How to Delete iPad Apps

When you have downloaded an application which you do not like or that you don't need again, you may delete it off your iPad. To do that, just press and keep your finger on the app icon till the icons begin jiggling about. You ought to then see an **X** at the top left corner of every icon.

Tap the **"x"** to dispose of the app. Do not worry; you cannot take away inbuilt apps on phone or contacts by doing this so that it won't cause any problem.

CHAPTER 7

How to Solve Slow iPad Problems

Is your iPad working slowly? Might it get bogged down after a couple of hours? At the same time as this is extra, not uncommon with old iPads that don't have the control power of the new iPad Air and iPad Pro Tablets, even the latest iPad can impede. A couple of multiple reasons just why an iPad could also begin operating slow, such as an application having troubles or a sluggish web connection. Thankfully, that is generally easy to revive.

- **First: stop all of your new apps**

One common reason behind an iPad to start chugging is a problem with the application itself instead of the iPad. If you enjoy a form that is working slower than usual, it could sound reasonable to go through the home button to close the application and re-launch it. However, pressing the home button wouldn't normally close out the app. It suspends the app, which mostly keeps it freezing in the backdground.

Some applications even continue steadily to run in the backdrop mode. Those are usually applications that stream music like Pandora, Spotify, or the melody app that is included with the iPad.

If the hassle is specifically with an individual app, we'll need to stop from it using the duty display. This may correctly close the application down and purge it from memory space, permitting you to release a 'fresh' version from it. Please discover that you might lose unsaved functions by exiting the app. If it's currently working on an objective, it could be better to make the application finishes the duty before proceeding.

Within the job screen, it is an excellent concept to have a summary of any applications that are taking part in music. It's not likely they may be causing a headache, or even if the application is loading the track from the web, it will not expend enough of your bandwidth to rely upon. However, last from the app won't hurt, and maybe sure the application isn't impacting something.

To shut the program, you will need to constitute a summary of all apps that will be operating in the background.

- **Double-click the home button in the bottom of your iPad.**

When you press it two times in quick succession, your most up to date applications are shown as cascading home windows across the screen. You might navigate via this screen by swiping from left-to-right or right-to-left.

The windows can have a related application icon above it.

***To close an app:

- Keep the finger down at the home display window.

- Without lifting your finger from the screen, swipe in the direction of the very best of the screen.

***This gesture resembles *"flicking"* the application from the iPad. Remember: you Tap the application windowpane, not the application icon.

Reboot the iPad

Closing the applications may not continuously do just fine. Within this example, rebooting the iPad is the product quality recourse. This will flush from memory and offer your iPad a fresh start.

NB: many humans believe the iPad forces down as the rest/wake button on the top right-hand corner of the iPad is pressed down or as the flap of their smart cover or bright case is closed, but this places the iPad in droop/suspend setting.

To reboot the iPad:

- Keep down the rest/wake button until instructions appear; letting you know to glide a button to power from the iPad.

- When you slip the button, the tablet will turn off, and the iPad's screen should go dark.

Wait around several seconds and then start the iPad up pressing down the rest/wake button once again. You'll first start to see the Apple brand logo design on the screen as well as your iPad need. Your iPad must run extra fast but, if it begins bogging down, retain in mind the apps that are running at that time. Once in a while, a single application can purpose the iPad to execute poorly.

Is your iPad still walking slower than you want?

Check your wireless connection

It could not be your iPad that is working sluggishly. It could be your mobile network.

You can attempt the internet speed of your Wi-Fi network by using an application like ***Ookla's Speedtest***. This application will send information to a remote server and then dispatches records back to the iPad, looking into each send and download rates of speed.

The usual Wi-Fi network in the U.S. Gets around 12 megabits-per-second (Mbps), though it is unusual to see rates of speed of 25+ Mbps. You possibly might not see plenty of the slowdown using your connection until it receives around 6 Mbps or significantly less. It is across the amount of bandwidth it requires to stream films and video.

If you're experiencing a headache with your Wi-Fi connection, try moving nearer to your router. If the pace increases, you might look at improving your Wi-Fi range. That's common in more prominent structures, but even a little home could have troubles.

Ensure you're updated to the latest version of iOS

iOS is the operating device working on the iPad. At precisely the same time as the best revise sometimes will positively sluggish the iPad down a little, it's always a great idea to perform the latest operating-system on device. Not handiest will this make sure that you have the most up to date efficiency tweaks, it additionally warranties you have present fixes for just about any protection problems.

Setup an ad-blocker

If you're mainly seeing a decline when surfing the internet in the safari internet browser, however, your web velocity is not sluggish, with the ability to be more an indicator of which webpages you're surfing than the iPad itself.

The more significant advertisements with a web page, the much longer it does take to load. Moreover, if some of those advertisements stall out, you might be left anticipating the web page to pop-up.

One fashion to this is to set up an advertisement blocker. Those widgets beautify the safari web browser by using disallowing advertisements to weight on the internet website. They make each for more straightforward reading and faster launching. Sites such as this one generate income from adverts, which means this is a balance you have to fight.

Flip off background app refresh

Background app refresh let applications to refresh their content even when you are not utilizing them. In this manner, Facebook might Tap base and retrieve articles in your post wall, or an information app may also fetch the newest articles.

However, this runs on your processing rate and your web connection, so that it can make the iPad to perform just a little slower. This usually isn't the theory cause, but if you frequently find the iPad working slow (and if the electric battery drains quickly), you must flip off background app refresh.

Showing off background application refresh:

- Head to your iPad's configurations.
- Choose **General** from the left-hand navigation menu.

- Tap the background application refresh.

- Tap the on/off slider near the top of the screen.

If you are nevertheless experiencing progressive speeds, there is certainly yet another factor you can do.

Clear STORAGE SPACE

If you're operating desperately low on space for storage, clearing up a little more room for the iPad can on occasion, improve efficiency. This will be achieved by deleting applications that you haven't used for quite a long time, particularly video games you don't play anymore.

It's clean to see which applications are employing the most space on your iPad:

1. Head to **Settings.**

2. Select **General** from the left-hand navigation menu.

3.   Tap **storage space & iCloud usage**.

4.   Tap **Manage Storage Space** (under the very best storage program). This may demonstrate which apps are using up the utmost storage.

You can additionally increase safari when you delete your cookies and internet background, although this might purpose you to log back to any websites that have saved your login records.

CHAPTER 8

How to Fix Used iPad that can't be Activate

If you buy a used iPad, it is interesting. In the end, you come with an iPad and stretch your budget by acquiring a used one, especially for individuals who are not economically buoyant.

Some individuals encounter this issue along the way of activating their new device: The iPad will inquire further for somebody else's Apple ID and wouldn't typically work unless supplied.

This isn't a challenge that can't be fixed, so do not fret because you'll get it fixed following these steps.

- It is consequently an attribute of Apple's Find my iPad service known as activation lock.

- Activation Lock is a security measure that Apple

raised to cope with the allergy of iPad thefts. In earlier years, if someone takes an iPad without blockage by lock feature, they could clean it, resell it, and breakout with the crime. Activation lock altered the situation.

- When the initial owner setup finds my iPad on the tool, the **Apple ID** used will be stored on Apple's activation servers together with almost every other information about the phone. The activation servers will most effectively unlock the phone again if that unique Apple ID can be used. If you no more have the Apple ID, you'll never be in a position to activate or use the tablet. This facilitates the security of your iPad because nobody would like to grab a tablet they can't use. On the other hand, it generally does not harm you if you recently procure the phone.

- Dealing with activation lock is annoying, but additionally, it is smooth to solve. It's mainly possible, and the prior consumer just forgot to carefully turn off find my iPad or erase the tool correctly before offering it on the market (though it could also be a sign you've purchased a stolen device, so be cautious).

- You should contact the preceding owner of the telephone for him/her to consider the necessary steps.

How to Remove Activation Lock on iPad

- It is expedient that you should unlock or remove activation lock from the acquired iPad (used iPad) by inputting the prior owners' **Apple ID.** This technique can be initiated by getting in contact with the owner and detailing the scenario.

- If the owner lives near to you, I'll recommend that you hand over the phone back to him/her with the mission to insert the mandatory unlock code which is his/her Apple ID. When the seller gets the iPad at hand, he/she only will enter the necessary Apple ID on the activation lock display. Having done such, restart the telephone and then forge forward with the typical activation process.

Ways to Remove Activation Lock using iCloud

Sometimes, things can get a bit messy and complicated if the merchant/seller cannot physically access the tablet thanks to circumstances such as distance among other factors. This may also be resolved effortlessly as the owner may use iCloud to eliminate the activation lock from the phone through his accounts by following the steps below:

- Visit iCloud.com on any device, either mobile or laptop.
- Log-on with the Apple ID he/she used to activate the telephone.
- Click Find My iPad.
- Select All Devices.
- Go through the iPad you sold or want to market.
- **Select Remove from Accounts.**

Having achieved that, after that, you can PULL THE PLUG ON the iPad, and you switch it ON again. After that, you can proceed with the standard activation process.

How to Fix Locked Home-Screen or Security

Password

If you activate your phone and find out either the iPad's home display screen or the security password lock display, therefore that the supplier/vendor didn't completely erase the smartphone before offering it for you. On this notice, you'll need the owner to wipe these devices to be able to do it with the activation process.

The next two procedures should be followed as you hand over the phone to the owner or seller to unlock the phone;

- If the tablet works on iOS 10 and later version, the owner has to log out of iCloud and subsequently erase these devices by heading *to Settings -> General -> reset -> Erase All Content* and *Settings.*

- If the tablet works on iOS 9, the seller/seller must go to *Settings -> General -> reset -> Erase All*

Content and *Settings* and enter his/her Apple ID when prompted.

- When the erase process is completed, you're absolving to activate your phone with no further ado or hold off.

How to Wipe an iPad Using iCloud

Imagine if you can't gain access to the vendor/merchant due to some reasons, yet you will need your mobile phone to be wiped entirely for easy convenience, the seller may use iCloud to erase it. This is attained by ensuring the phone you want to get triggered linked to a WiFi network or mobile data network, and then inform the seller to follow along with the next steps:

- Visit http://iCloud.com/#find

- Sign in with the Apple id he/she applied to the

phone that is with you or sold to you.

- Click *All Devices*.

- Choose the phone sold you or available to you.

- Select *Erase iPad*.

- When the phone is erased, click *Remove from Accounts*.

- Restart the phone, and you are all set.

How to Erase an iPad Using Find My iPad App

This process is very much indeed identical to the approach explained above using iCloud by just using the Find my iPad application installed on some other iPad device. If the owner prefers to get this done, connect the phone you're buying to Wi-Fi or mobile data, and then inform the owner to adhere to the steps below:

- Start the *find my iPad* app.

- Sign on with the Apple ID they applied to the phone sold to you.

- Choose the phone.

- Tap *Actions*.

- Tap *Erase iPad*.

- Tap *Erase iPad* (It is the same button, however on a new display).

- Enter *Apple ID*.

- Tap *Erase*.

- Tap *Remove from Accounts*.

  - Restart the iPad and get started doing the setup process.

CHAPTER 9

How exactly to Watch Television on your own iPad

Among the exquisite issues about the iPad is for you to use the Tablet for viewing TV. There are a few appropriate alternatives that support you to view Television on your iPad, and that means you don't have to miss your preferred show or any big game.

Many of these devices functions by intercepting its transmission out of your wire package and then broadcasting it through your wi-fi network, that enables you to access your shows from any place in the home even though on the run via your iPad's data connection.

However, one thrilling option converts the iPad into a lightweight TV, and if you do not want to invest the money on expensive add-ons or accessories, sometimes an application is all you have to.

@TV Plus

Belkin is the newest manufacturer to leap into the market place, and their @TV is priced among the volcano glide and the Slingbox Slingplayer. It offers all precisely the same primary functions of both products, which include the ability to pause and record live TV.

One feature oddly lacking from @TV can be an HDMI connection. @TV best uses an element or amalgamated cables instead of the better acceptable HDMI.

TiVo Stream

If you're not thinking about cutting the cable, TiVo could be the best answer for pressing your television sign to your iPad. Sadly, it might be the most luxurious, at least beforehand charges. You'll either want to include a TiVo stream device on your existing TiVo set up, or you will require the TiVo Roamio Plus, which include both TiVo Roamio for essential TiVo supplier and the TiVo motion for loading throughout the internet.

However, while getting set up on TiVo is more expensive, you might forestall renting an HD Dvd movie recorder from your wire issuer, which may be helping you save money.

The huge bonus to TiVo stream is the ability to watch recorded shows in addition to concert events. The flow fundamentally turns your iPad into a TiVo player, which means you get access to the whole great deal documented on your TiVo's DVR.

Sling TV

The war to cut the cord has been waging for a couple of

years now, but when sling TV surfaced, the tide officially started to be towards the cable companies. Sling TV is not a tool that throws your current day cable indicators to your Television or an antenna that accumulates channels for your iPad. It's an online cable company, due to this, they do precisely the same simple process that your wire organization will, without strolling wire to your dwelling. Instead, you stream your channels throughout the internet. Sling provides you with the usage of popular stations like ESPN, AMC, TNT, TBS as well as others. You can additionally sign up to HBO, Epix, and further channel packages.

The very best part is that sling TV needs to forget about hardware to work. The terrible part is that it will not broadcast local stations.

Cable Television / Network Apps

A chance to starting up hardware on your entertainment device or plugging an antenna into the iPad is downloading applications from your Wire Company or primary networks.

Many major companies like COX TV, Time Warner Cable, and DirectTV offer applications for the iPad, and that means you can watch TV, even though not all support the full total range of TV provided through your subscription rather than all provision ability to stream over 3G/4G/5G.

You could additionally access top-class articles via apps, with a few restrictions based on your issuer. HBO, Cinemax, Showtime and Starz all have applications that utilize a few providers.

Beyond reputable applications from your wire issuer or top quality channels, there are a few remarkable applications for streaming films and TV. The two most popular choices are **Netflix**, which gives an excellent selection of movies and Television for a comparatively low subscription charge, and **Hulu Plus**, which doesn't have precisely the same movie series but offers a few Television shows still within the present-day season.

Crackle is likewise an excellent choice for loading movies and will not require any membership charges.

Slingbox Slingplayer

No more to be confused with Sling TV, Slingbox's Slingplayer works via intercepting the TV signal away off your wire box and "slinging" it across your home network. The Slingplayer software transforms one's body into a good deal that enables you to stream it to your iPad across both Wi-Fi as well as your iPad's 3G/4G/5G data connection. Using the Slingplayer app, you can listen to other stations watching any television screen that you can view at home. You can also gain access to your DVR watching recorded shows.

Beyond being truly a very significant way to view remotely, Slingplayer is also an incredible solution for people who want usage of the television in virtually any room inside without connecting wire or springing for two televisions. One drawback would be that the iPad application should be bought individually and provides an incredible chunk onto the charge of these devices.

CHAPTER 11

How to Extend iPad's Battery Life

With every iPad release, one continuous point remains. The iPad is now faster, and the images get better every year. Nevertheless, the device works with the first 10 hours of battery life. However, also for those individuals that use their iPad 24hrs each day, it's still easy for it to perform. Moreover, there is nothing worse than looking to stream video from Netflix and then have that low battery message pop-up and interrupt your show.

Thankfully, there are a few tips you could utilize to keep iPad battery life and hold that from happening as often.

Concealed secrets that will change you into an iPad expert:

Right here's how you can get the best of your iPad's battery life span:

- **Adjust the brightness:** The iPad comes with an automatic-brightness feature which facilitates the iPad predicated on the light quality within the area, but this program isn't always enough. Modifying the overall lighting could be the first solitary thing you can do to help ease out a little more from your battery consumption. You can transform the light by starting the iPad's configurations, choosing screen & view from the left-side menu and moving the brightness slider. The goal is to get it to a stage where it's nevertheless comfortable enough to learn, however nearly as shiny as the default establishing.

- **Switch off Bluetooth:** Most of us haven't any Bluetooth devices linked to the iPad, so all the Bluetooth carrier does for all of us is waste charge of the iPad's battery life. When you have no Bluetooth devices connected, ensure Bluetooth is switched off. A brief way to turn the transfer for Bluetooth off is to open up the iPad manager - panel by swiping up from the backside of the screen.

- **Switch off Location services:** At precisely the same time as even the Wi-Fi version of the iPad will do a fantastic job of identifying its location, most people do not use the location service on our iPad as much as we utilize them on our iPad. Turning OFF GPS is a concise and clean manner to save lots of a little battery even while not quitting any feature. Also, remember if you need to use GPS, you may switch it **ON**. You can switch off location services in the iPad's configurations below privacy.

- **Turn off notification:** While notification is an excellent feature, it can drain a small amount of battery life because the tool assessments to check on if it needs to force a notification to the screen. If you want to do the most to optimize your battery life, you can turn drive notification off completely. You could likewise turn it off for specific apps, reducing all of the push notifications you obtain. You may switch off notification in configurations.

- **Fetch email less regularly:** With default configurations, the iPad will check out brand spanking new email each quarter-hour. Pushing this back to a half-hour or one hour can help your battery last much longer. Move to configurations, choose the email settings and select the "fetch new data" choice. This will enable you to set how often your iPad fetches email. There could even be a choice only to have check email manually.

- **Switch off 4G:** More often than not, we use the iPad at home, this means the use from it via our mobile data connection on. We utilize it at home exclusively. If you regularly end up low on battery, a good suggestion is to turn off your 4G data connection. This may protect it from draining any power when you are not using it.

- **Turn off background application refresh:** Background app refresh keeps your apps up to date by relaxing them even while the iPad is idle or as long as you're on various other apps. This may drain a little extra battery strength. Get into configurations, choose General configurations and scroll down till you find "background app refresh." You can choose to turn off the service or certainly flip off specific apps you don't want to run in the background.

- **Discover apps consuming your battery:** Do you realize you could test thoroughly your iPad's battery usage? That is a fantastic manner to find what applications you're using the most and which apps can be consuming more than their expected percentage of your battery. You could test utilization within the iPad's configurations by choosing battery from the left-hand side menu.

- **Match iPad improvements:** It's continuously important to keep iOS updated to the latest from

Apple. Not merely would this help optimize the battery life of the iPad, it also ensures you're getting the latest security fix and patching any bugs that have popped up, which allows the iPad run efficiently.

- **Reduce Animation:** That is a technique to save a little of battery life and make the iPad show up a bit more reactive. The iPad's user interface consists of a few animations like glass windows zooming in and zooming out, and the parallax influence on icons, which makes them seem to hover over the backdrop picture. You can turn off those user interface effect by heading to **Settings**, Tapping **General Settings**, Tap **Display,** and getting to reduce animation to get it turned **Off**.

- **Buy a Smart Case:** The smart case can save battery life by placing the iPad into **Sleep mode** when you close the flap. It might not look like a great deal of conservation, however in case you aren't with the habit of striking the rest/wake button each time you have completed using the iPad; it could help offer you a supplementary five, ten or even quarter-hour extension of battery strength by the end of the day.